TEARS THAT SPILL GOD

Water For My Seeds
Rooting For You, On My Side of the Hill
Tears That Spill God

Thierra Walker

Copyright © 2025 by Thierra Walker

All rights reserved. No part of this book may be used or reproduced by any means, graphic, electronic, or mechanical, including photocopying, recording, taping, or by any information storage retrieval system, without the written permission of the publisher except in the case of brief quotations embodied in critical articles and reviews.

It was time to start dealing with my shit I had lingering. To take inventory on the pain I've stacked in corners like books. To admit the clutter still cornered me more than it should. The idea of deep cleaning often invites fear of what could shift and rattle my heart in ways I worked to forget. I lost sight of the whole purpose of life: to make a million small deaths within myself. *That's how I know I'm winning (healing).* There lies my authenticity every time I dare to pinch a layer to peel back, pushing myself to uncomfortable places. To accept that nothing is lost in an illusionary world we live in, it just changes form, and I can then wrap my heart with the knowing that nothing is missing, ever. I am on my journey to expose all the human shit I've accumulated and "bought into" about myself over the years and see it for what it is - to get it off me, to get it out of me by any means. *Light as a feather is the goal.* What's that saying we all love to say ? *"I am in it but not of it."* Having a human experience is challenging enough- yet most of what we're attached to is trivial and that alone is a death to come to. To deal with all the things that could possibly pull you back and keep you stuck - that's that graduate level work. *I salute the ones trying.* I have no expectations for what I hope is gained and received as nothing I say is gospel or all-knowing for your experience. However, I do invite you to reflect on what you're shifting out of and stepping into with these pages to follow. We are as brilliant as we are authentic, catching all curved balls with praying hands.

Life is nothing but a test of heart- how heavy are you?

To feel deeply is true power. To let it transform you is gained wisdom.

TABLE OF CONTENTS

DEPARTURE: HOME IS THE HEART	1
TRAIN STOPS: 28 CHAPTERS	3
GROWING TREES IN GOOD TIME	4
BURNING HOUSES	6
LOVE AT AWKWARD ANGLES	8
LOVE, SEX, NARCISSISM	14
LEVELED MIND BRINGS HIGHER INSIGHTS	18
I PRAY YOU MAKE IT HOME	20
CAN'T CRY WOLF	22
SILENT SHEDDING	24
LOST LOVE LETTERS	26
I LET A WAR CRY SING	30
SITUATIONSHIPS	32
GRAY AREAS GET INTERESTING	36
A BITTER BAR	40
FLOWERS FOR REGINA	44
GOOD GRIEF	48
DARK HOURS	52

FUCK / AGAIN	56
ALCHEMY	60
HOW MANY DEATHS DO WE HAVE IN A LIFETIME?	64
TODAY, I GOT BY	68
FINDING BALANCE	70
I WROTE THIS LISTENING TO *POUND CAKE* BY DRAKE	74
LOVE DON'T ALWAYS SPIN THE BLOCK	76
LET US LIGHT SOME SAGE	80
RUBBERBAND PROBLEMS	86
ONGOING NOTHINGNESS	90
PAY YOUR RESPECTS	96
ARRIVAL: NEW JOYS, OLD LOVES	100

DEPARTURE: HOME IS THE HEART

So much stuff is dying as I write this book.
I buried so much in these pages. I gave them a place to rest. My mind is no longer a pit stop for unwanted thoughts.
It was time I let them go.
Time to liberate us both into a love that can hold us and meet us where we are this time.
I have no hate or resentment, just discernment on knowing when it's time to end one cycle.
Nothing is lost, nothing is missing.
We're blessed and we appreciate the blessings.
I am uncomfortable, and that's okay.
Being uncomfortable is just an invitation to choose growth and take inventory on what my heart is ready to let go of.
And every time I do, my home is replenished.
And whatever didn't make it past my doorstep,
it's all love.
And whatever made it inside but couldn't stay,
it was nice when it was.
I am learning to be more intentional now.

More aware of who falls into the category of:
"Kids can play in the yard but not in the house."
Or, as my Grandmom would say:
"We not playing that running in and out. Either you inside or you outside."

I am learning subtle lessons later than I'd like to.
The ones where I should know better, but I haven't mastered how to fully execute it when it counts, so here we are — *again*. I like to live with the

thought that if we have the desire to move forward, become better, and grow with an open, pure heart,
we're the winning ones.
It's all about your heart presence.
No matter how many detours and unexpected turns,
I am always on time for the timing of my life.

Everything is as it should be.

Deep breaths. Long exhales.

TRAIN STOPS: 28 CHAPTERS

GROWING TREES IN GOOD TIME

The in-between. The no longer, but not quite. Remaining excited for the new space being called upon me. Making new moves. Some wise, some still dumb. But we grow trees in good time.

I'm always right on time. Always where I'm meant to be, eventually at least. I end up in blessed positions, despite staying in shittier ones because my heart reflects love itself. That's the only way. That's how I know under the bullshit, my foundation is solid. My trees got something of depth to stand on. I'm rooted by my heartstrings. Loving to love, I be love drunk, forgetting intuition is authority. But life is funny like that. I guess that's how we evolve. Eventually, we get tired of falling so much, the ground gives us a courtesy boost. We start to see shit differently.

How we can be better.
How we're always learning, growing, healing.
How to better care for ourselves.
How to *do* better and not just *know* better.
How to bridge that gap.
How to be at peace while waiting.
How to live in joy while the world is fucking sad.
How to scale back and tap into our own inner world.
But in good time, at the perfect time, you'll reach where you're going cause them seeds been planted.

BURNING HOUSES

I was never good at being sad.
I always seem to let it take me too far.
I weep rivers beneath my feet,
Losing my head in the storm, so deep I'd rather drown than stand in this burning house.
Scary when you find yourself chasing folks rather than take another loss of a home built in someone else.
But you can bring me all the pain,
I know my way out.
I can clean up the mess, I be a mess myself.
I come from a family where the women burn holes in their chests for niggas burning holes in their pockets.
Always falling for the okey doke for empty promises but we found a way to dance in our sorrow so the pain don't mean shit by the sun-up.
See, we were never good at being sad, we just got used to burning houses.

LOVE AT AWKWARD ANGLES

There are hard things I had to learn that put me in uncomfortable situations: Sometimes we can't see patterns from our perspective, so we suffer from all angles until enough self-awareness is practiced.

Once you arrive to a place of balance, retrospect is always the sweet spot, but it takes time and spiritual discipline to free yourself in ways only you can know to be important. It invites the potential for grief and pain, as some situations we love may not love us back in the way to birth life into us.

Some love just drains us, some unions are just toxic, and some situations are dead ends, but we grow as the reward. We get better for ourselves. Our spirits grow ten times, heart richer.

The greatest path to self-wealth is an open heart. When pain takes our ass for a ride, it rips us apart, we bleed for what feels like an eternity in every moment. The strength of softness and surrender is revealed. We fall into our greatest healing. The one that took years to get to.

And this time, we choose it. We not running from it. We running home.

Stop trying to make it make sense.
When we release the need to know why things played out the way they did, we free ourselves.

The explanation doesn't minimize the hurt.

What happened, happened. Move different.

Someone once told me something profound that I only just digested in this moment.

She said, *"How are you going to move regardless? How are you going to move for yourself?"*

I always based how I moved forward on how they chose to recognize the issue, rectify my pain, or release me. It was always an afterthought, after I studied how they were moving. I never took authority for my own knowing and what I needed, despite my feelings.

I let my feelings and ego dictate or justify my inability to just go forward.

I want to give people the benefit of the doubt so bad that I kept leaving the door cracked, hoping they'll take the opportunity to show me that they're apologetic or understand where they wronged me just so I can keep them around or not fully close the door on them completely.

That was my lack of boundaries and lack of self-respect. I kept allowing people to play with me. I kept letting the manipulation take over my value. I allowed myself to be half of an existence for an ounce of their love.

My heart knew what I went through. I don't need to justify my experience of the trauma to outsiders to clear my name or perfect their perspective of me. When you're a good person, you leave a mark on people; when people are hurting, they leave stains. *Two different things.*

Live at the height of yourself. May your worth stack up.

We are responsible for our own healing. It is on us to do and be better for ourselves. I had to learn to stop giving my power away by wanting them to acknowledge my feelings and understand me. I kept fighting uphill battles, thinking that was the price of a solid love. In hindsight I was just looking for excuses to still deal with them. Telling myself we have unfinished business to keep the story replaying, to keep my emotions invested when spirit kept trying to steer me away. Disrespect is the final straw, not the opportunity to give them a chance to explain themselves in hopes they will change my mind about what I know to be true from my experience. All history with someone isn't good history, and that can't keep me stuck.

I must be at peace with moving forward for my healing without acknowledgment, and that has been the hardest thing to do. Free myself without validation from the one who hurt me. Having to take accountability for both parties because we all know true apologies can only come from those who take real responsibility, not from those who seek to benefit themselves.

I free myself when I take ownership of my pain, because I now shift the power back into my own hands and make myself the consistent companion. In turn, I release them back to wherever they belong. My calling is higher than my circumstance.

May I remind myself that the work is never done but the work must be in progress or all I'll be doing is transferring weight without cutting the fat.

I can't afford to stay stuck in cycles that recycle people with different lies — same game, different strategy. I peep it now for what it is. Can't even be mad at it because some shit is just in someone's nature. Be easy. As human as we are to want revenge, we must be conscious enough to know that revenge is ill to the heart and never holds more weight than a mind living with guilt and shame. Let that be enough.

Nothing is ever wasted, just course-corrective. Enjoy that shit for what it is.

GROWING PAINS:
ONE TEACHES
YOU WHERE A CHANGE
NEEDS TO BE MADE,
AND ONE TEACHES
YOU WHERE
NOT TO REJECT
YOURSELF
FOR ANYONE OR
ANYBODY.

LOVE, SEX, NARCISSISM

I love the most when I'm hurt.

Real love is how you move when it's over. I used to think it meant something when you came back - like you finally saw my value- but maybe I was only easy access. Maybe I'm just where you want to be because you'd rather not be over there until you get on your feet.

We somehow struggled our way through turmoil and disrespect. We romanticized that into meaning something. We glorified the moments of verbal abuse spewed at one another because we both knew the passion that came afterward was the only thing that saved us. It was the only thing we had left. We're more alike than we think. We both just want love, we just want to feel loved, so when we create that fantasy around someone, we can't just let it go. We save fantasy before we save ourselves.

Ain't that how it goes? We be forgetting that people and permanency are not mutually exclusive. We fight for it even if we are killing ourselves for the crumbs. We're both hurting, we're both in pain. We're both traumatized. Both for different reasons, which brought us together because appreciation did exist between us at one point. Now, it's all lies, sex, and attachment. Sounds really good on a late night when you want to be laid up, but it's nothing more than this back-and-forth dance we're doing that ain't going nowhere. We've gone as far as spirit will allow us to.

Perhaps I've outgrown that season, and you pretended you didn't for your benefit.

In the end, all we want to feel is loved. Cared about. Seen. Heard. Talked to with kindness when upset. Someone to be loyal to us. To have our backs. Even if it comes with an end date—not everything that comes is stamped with forever but what we learn is. We want to feel valued in our absence. We want to know that our time together will forever be special and not forgotten or overwritten. You destroyed that feeling for me.

For a while I felt safe with you, because even though we weren't good, I always knew romance and intimacy was reserved for us.

There was some safety in that.

I was loyal to you. I had my shit, but I was here. I never used the "we not together" to justify stupidity. Sex ain't just sex to me—that's sacred intimacy. The way you mold your body to fit into mine – man, I thought I was special. I thought what we had was something special. I don't know if that hurts more or the fact that I let myself get swept up against my better judgment.

It always teaches more than it hurts. Remember that.

Looking dumb is the price you pay when you go against intuition. It happens though. I play it off because my feelings don't matter over yours. How can they? You keep score on who hurt who, so how I feel will never be heard. You'll always twist it to justify your actions, saying if I hadn't done this, you wouldn't have done that. You such a charming narcissist, but ain't that how it goes? The tit for tat instead of leaving is your biggest downfall. Getting mad at me for the very things you do—you love a double standard, huh? You know you tired when you just want a motherfucka to leave you alone, yo. Leave me where I'm at. But I'll never stay where you left me.

I sometimes think you like hurting me because, in some twisted way, you think you teaching me the principle. Shit, once you can't mentally break me down, you withdraw emotionally. The push and pull, you punish me when you're hurting. It's like we both gotta be fucked up for you to feel an ounce of joy. Communication was never our strong suit. We just get mad, don't talk, come back weeks later, kiss and fuck because that's the only closeness we had left. Truth is, we feel so alone with each other, but the pain feels so familiar it keeps us bound. But I don't blame you. You do what you're allowed.

I thought I was well beyond vacant self-love.

I had enough. Your ego couldn't let go of the idea of me. It would make sense why you would always say, "Let's go back to the beginning." I was genuinely here holding onto you—to this—even when you weren't. Seems you only held on because other people you had lined up ain't do it for you, or you weren't ready to be done with that version of me in your head. It was never about me—not the real me.

Truth is, there's so much shit in between you and me to ever be something significant. We killed that dream, ran it in the ground. I tried hard to love you, but maybe it just wasn't supposed to be that hard. Maybe that's the whole point I keep fucking missing.

Letting go ain't easier either. What do I do when it hurts when you're gone but I'm killing myself to be okay when you're here? **I take the honorable road to saving myself and clearing my energy. That's law.** *It all points back to self every time.*

LEVELED MIND BRINGS HIGHER INSIGHTS

True joy is not dependent on physical sight, just as rooted faith sees beyond our current understanding. Divine order always exceeds perspective until lessons are collected to unlock the gift of hindsight. But do remember, things are always working for you, even when they seem to be working against you. Nothing is ever good or bad, it just is, as the meanings we give things change. Control is forever an illusion; be it out of your hands, let it be so. If it's above you, pray it up. Let yourself be surprised with the re-route.

I PRAY YOU MAKE IT HOME

The path isn't a straight shot to your destination, rather a devoted commitment to finding your way. We often doubt our greatness in the period of waiting, but this past year has shown me that I still have value even when I'm tripping over my own feet. That I am still powerful even in the quiet hours. Protection still covers me, I'm just figuring it out, finding my way. Stumbling onto new paths, because who knew painful mistakes can lead to beautiful places—the space where I'm not quite the same, but I am certainly not where I'd like to be in this season of my life. Knowing that the scale always increases for what we see for ourselves. Where I'm learning to embrace my fuckups because now, I know what it means to walk my own truth. To fully forgive myself for my past and any time I've acted out of fear, manipulation, and lack. Those dense energies were never mine.

Even if I don't know everything. We find our way. We figure it out. We do our best. There's God in the wait. God in the unknown. God in the ugly. God in the gray. In the relapses. Wherever you are, God is. Even if we forget our godliness within ourselves. It's all beautiful, even when it doesn't make sense. I lost my head but found my heart. Finding balance within myself. Making peace with where I am. That is the flow to be in.

You must get to a place where you do this life shit for you. Fuck what anyone else thinks, as long as you proud of it, keep going, and keep getting better. Release the human shit.

Feel how you feel, just end with love.

CAN'T CRY WOLF

She was the first person who made me freeze every time I looked in her eyes.

She asked me, "Do you not look in people's eyes?" I replied, "I do, but it's never nothing there, it's never this hard. Nothing behind them."

That made me stop and think: Do I not see people because I'm not emotionally available, or do I go toward people who aren't emotionally available because, deep down, I don't feel like I deserve love? Or maybe, is it that I see the depth in someone else's eyes, and I can't handle it, because now I'm actually opening myself up to myself and what I deserve, and that's new for me?

If everything reflects self, I have no choice but to take accountability for the mirrors around me.

We all reflect one another, so maybe at that time I just wasn't ready to see anybody or see my own shit. I guess at a certain level, if we're all mirrors, can only see others as deeply as we want to see ourselves. You choose the same until you are ready to choose different. When you feel like you're not good enough, you stay in shit longer by validating yourself through a relationship. We cling to the bullshit, until we're ready to see ourselves and ask why we keep tolerating dead things. Toxic things.

Can't blame anyone else for betraying your own intuition. I tend to look at the good in people and I magnify it -I focus on what I want to grow; I want to bring that quality out in them, make them see it for themselves. But realistically, let's just call it what it is—saving niggas. I be saving niggas before I save myself. *And in this life- you can only save yourself.* Can't cry wolf when it's you. All about moving with love, but you can't always move solely because of love.

Spirit is always rewarded when you honor your intuition.

SILENT SHEDDING

I'm craving to touch and feel something familiar. I'm sad because it feels like everything around me is new, but there is nothing new. Maybe it's me, maybe I'm the stranger in my own body because I've never held myself with this regard before. *I got some nerve now.* To hold myself higher like I did the people I used to love, or that I still do but *they not touching me now.* I've outgrown them. I feel me changing, and I don't know how to identify with myself. I'm learning me all over again. So no, I can't put my finger on it. I'm sad but I can't cry. It's like a silent shedding. A beautiful, beautiful ceremony with myself and spirit.

I place a bucket of shame on my back every day. Without giving relief of the thought that maybe things just happen the way they are supposed to. Realizing that my shadow still needs more love- my subconscious thoughts cripple me at times. I believe that if I can fix it, then I have control. That if I carry all the blame, then the solutions must be in reach. That I can change the outcome. Change the dynamic. Change the ending. I stay falling into the projections that people have of me to prove I am a "good" person. I hate the feeling that makes us believe if we choose ourselves we are disappointing people especially when you're exhausted from avoiding yourself. It's not so much if you are a good person to them, but are you being good to yourself? Or are you storing mad shit within?

I cannot hold myself to how people perceive me, especially when I have grown from that. I'm okay with not being who I thought I was in regard to other people's perspectives. Nothing to take personally about myself, but something to remember. It's not my burden to carry. I did what I could, whether they thought it was good or bad. But what is good or bad? The pendulum just swings in my favor, as everything happens for a reason.

I know my heart, I know it. When I do things from the heart, it's always right. When I feel from the heart, it's always right. When I see from the heart, it's always right. But when I feel from the heart, I tend to keep people who only want to keep a *version* of me. Maybe because that small percentage that they magnify - feels massive- because I'm still learning to amplify my own existence. Let situations carry themselves instead of me trying to fix things.

LOST LOVE LETTERS

Dear Old Lover,

When I think about you, I give the thought so much gratitude. I could blame you for how we ended up, but the best gift you've ever given me was sight. The gift of seeing myself through constructive lenses. To see what I needed to work on for myself. You taught me a lot about myself, even though we might have been destructive along the way. I feel we held onto each other because we had the same heart if you peeled back the trauma. We wanted the same thing. We just wanted to love each other. We didn't understand why it had to be so hard, but we kept trying for the vision.

I'll forever love you for seeing that with me, even if we never reached it. I learned a lot along the way about my own world, how I tend to operate in it, and how it leaves the ones I love around me to feel small, undervalued, and disrespected. To step outside of my perspective to see someone else's was never my forte. I *heard* it but it never trumped mine.

I always thought my way was the right way because my love was so big for you. I couldn't understand why you couldn't see it my way, you couldn't understand why I couldn't listen, both leaving us on the outs with each other. There was no equal give and take, no balance, no compromise, the cat and mouse game, too much chasing each other when all we had to do was stand there in love.

I hope you know I loved you. I know projections were painted on blank slates, but when you call a love to you and it comes, you get scared. You find it hard to trust it because of how much shit you have been through to get there. But I let this be a lesson moving forward, to not fear what I want, to not fear love. To not fear loving myself. To not lose myself even when it feels like home in someone. To regulate my own emotions. To soothe my own pain so it doesn't bleed on the ones I love. To love fearlessly, even if it doesn't stay, because it's about the experience. I am grateful to have experienced you. However this next chapter unfolds between you and I, gratitude will be held next to your name.

I release you to stay. I release you to go. I release you to see you happy, however that looks for you.

WITH LOVE, T

Things can still be tender.
That doesn't mean you're still stuck on them though.

I LET A WAR CRY SING

I let a war cry sing. I let it ripple through bone. Just enough to give rise. Had to let it be known that I'm proving my strength by not holding myself in suffering. That I didn't need to do that any longer. That it's okay to be the bad guy, by way of loving on me. We all do it in our own way. Therefore, I cannot blame or shame another with the same dedication. It's all in the game. A different part played; another side taken. We all let our war cry sing. And sing. And sing.

SITUATIONSHIPS

I don't handle gray areas well.
My mind works in absolutes, either you in or out.
See, we set up different.
If I love you, I love you. I don't leave, I don't quit.
But you did.
How we so bad for one another,
But we're so good when we want each other.
I hear what you saying, but I won't stay put for you to come back to.
I can't do that to myself.
I can't willfully keep myself stuck.
Too much life waiting.
And sitting in limbo won't do it for me.

Know your place,
know your worth,
know what
you bring to the table.

GRAY AREAS GET INTERESTING

We're in between seasons, I'm in between feelings.
Lately, I'm unsure of myself.
Can't tell which version of me is left.
Somehow life seems to body me,
yet I'm still not grounded enough.
Going through the motions without solid footing,
the same thoughts I keep trying to overstep.
I can feel myself watching from the outside
slipping back, repeating tracks.
Maybe spirit wants me to be still,
but I don't do stillness well.
I don't sit pretty.
Waiting is too strenuous for how active I can get.
Going through the motions for the sake of going.
Destination not known, but there's beauty in lost moments.
I am allowing myself to change,
Allowing things to happen and part ways in the process.
Extending grace for endings is still a work in progress,
but we let die what's been long dead.
Even if it's me.

It's okay to mourn
someone longer
than they mourn you.

Spirit just want
me to flow
Spirit just wanna
stay close
Spirit is all that I know.
Spirit is closer
than close.
Spirit don't sit
well with you.
Spirit said it's time to go.

A BITTER BAR

How am I still being questioned on how solid I am,
when you don't want me?
You go off and do your own thing,
and you still expecting my loyalty.
Let me go out, you mad with me.
Your actions don't line up.
You good for the mind games,
then we all laid up and in love.
Before we argue again over the same things.

The work is to find
the gift in the
grief, that's
how you'll transmute it.

The transitional moments are the sweet spot between you, God, and the next level of yourself.

FLOWERS FOR REGINA

I heard my mother crying in the shower this morning. I quickly shut my eyes, as if she could see me hearing her.

A moment I'm sure she thought was private.

It's a hard thing to console a grieving parent, let alone comfort a parent who has no parents. Is it true that as you get older, the more you see your parents as friends rather than the ones who are supposed to have answers? Her voice echoed from the shower, as her tears rippled from room to room, spreading a familiar sadness.

Death was nothing new to our family. It came like clockwork, every January. Top of the year. As a reminder to us all, time to get uncomfortable again. Time to release, to surrender to our faith in the midst of heartache, confusion and rage. I look back, and all I see are old shells of all the versions I used to be. I still don't know how to trust I'll be okay, let alone believe myself when I say it'll all work out, even though it always does. I often wonder if I'm doing enough to usher ease in for my mother. Just as you find solid ground, on to the next refinement of self.

Death is tricky like that—be it someone else's or your own funeral. I'm either withering away with it or choosing to be reborn through it. Both hurt. Both, a process. Both, not easy. But only one is beautiful.

I hope for my mother to choose the latter. To choose life. She deserves all things beautiful. If God could grant me one thing, I'd ask for the sun to shine its brightest on her. To magnify her light just bright enough to bring remembrance to her resilience, to her warrior spirit. May you give your softest love to your strongest warriors.

We need it most.

We cannot bring life back to dead things, we are not God in that way. But I do pray to a God that knows my heart and a life that comes beyond grief.
One beyond its time.

GOOD GRIEF

To know loss is to know there is no timeline present. Grief is an entity of its own, coming and going when it's ready. Intolerant to haste. To condemn your sadness only gives rise to its blues, for the competition between ego and healing only breeds more sorrows. It's true, the end has arrived. Just as new life echoes in your emptiness. May you part in peace from those who've departed by choice. Do not dispose your worth simply because the wrong hands could not keep you.

Never prepared for grief, always prepared to mourn.

Is there an art to grieving?

> Where you feel endings in such a way that remind you how beautiful your expansion is called to be. That every time you are pulled from someone or something you love it's because growth is now calling you to pick a higher path.

> Where you sit deeply in pain to emerge higher in wisdom. Where loss is only a shedding to bring forth more light. More of yourself. Where grief is but an interesting path toward more freedom. To more trust.

> There's power in feeling a hurt that rattles you past comprehension only if you choose to fix your eyes on how great God can be.

Healing never makes sense until you're able to get your head just enough above water.

Am I not owed
the joy that life
still has for me?

DARK HOURS

These walls permeate death, casting shadows I don't care to see. My bed hugs my imprint. I lay lifeless, disregarding the sun as it dances across my bedroom floor. I'm filled with the thought of who might miss me if I skip next morning's sunrise. Will I get noticed for my absence, or the peace I've been praying for? I repeatedly utter, "God, I think you're mistaking me for one of your soldiers." This weight exceeds my rank. There is no fortitude left in this fight. My faith is in need of a miracle.

I condemned myself, carrying guilt over people parting ways for things not working out. Begging, apologizing, fixing, obsessing, worrying, punishing myself over my mistakes wouldn't change what's meant to be for me. Had I had more trust in myself, I could have carried my pain much quicker than overanalyzing ever could. Even in the midst of not understanding why some things must be removed, trust is and only ever is, the side to rest upon.

I suppose once you're ready to listen to intuition, you finally stop ignoring what innately feels wrong. You begin to brace yourself for the inevitable. You slowly start to realize that blessings don't come to these parts unless you part ways with where you're stuck.

Sometimes, I don't know what hurts most: someone who can't make up their mind about me, or myself for forgetting who the fuck I am.

I stand at the feet of myself.
I bow with reverence.
I be in awe of myself.
I'm so damn happy to be myself.

I'm honored to know myself.
I do this life shit in honor of myself.
I do things that will honor my health.
I do things that feel good to me.
I change my mind if need be.

I am my own savior
I stay empowered.
I let you go,
cut you off to honor new movement.

Cutting ties, no remorse,
that's how that go when it start feeling forced.

I honor myself.

FUCK / AGAIN

Fuck, my payment declined again.
Fuck, I'm sad again.
Fuck, I'm high again.
Fuck, my head hurts.
Fuck, I've been rejected again.
Fuck, I'm stuck in my head again.

Fuck, I'm still in this bed.
Fuck, I'm wanting her again.
Fuck, I want to paint again.
Fuck, I need to write again.
Fuck, I should start therapy again.
Fuck, I don't want to talk about all this shit again.
Fuck it, I'll be cool like always.
Fuck, my stomach hurts again.
Fuck, my heart is in my stomach now.
Fuck, I'm losing my mind again.
Fuck, I'm jealous now.
Fuck, I need to get out the fckn house, yo.
Fuck, I miss her though.
Fuck, I look like going back again.
Fuck, no.

Fuck, how long does heartbreak last again?
Fuck, when does happiness pull up?
Fuck, when my niggas pulling up again?
Fuck, old patterns and bad habits again.
Fuck, can we have sex again?
Fuck—just once—again?

Fuck it, these tears spill God anyway.

Have I arrived?
Am I all right?
God is on my side.
Ima be all right.

Here's a new day.
Ima be all right.
Ima get it right.
God is on my side.

Ima be cool.
Ima be okay
one moment at a time,
tryna have a good day.

ALCHEMY

Life is nothing but alchemy, turning the worst of things for the better. To shape pain instead of folding for it. To make it sit beneath our feet. Everything is art, even the way we hurt. Might as well make the ride beautiful. I've come to learn that, even with my many pieces, no one and nothing can break me into anything smaller than I make myself. I really need to stop that shit. Life is a process of doing epic shit before visitation hour is over. May we live the hours to live for ourselves.

It's always easier to talk on top of the mountain when you're beyond the valley, but I'm allowing myself to learn the graceful dance between happy and sad, love and loss, grief and gratitude. I'm not rushing either–because life is easier on me when I let things be. No force, no control, allowing the rest to spill over into some new shit for me. I deserve that much.

Today it can all seem so simple, then tomorrow be a riddle. It be like that.

I'm getting better with welcoming the reflection of the lesson rather than fixating on the ending of something beautiful. But the worst parts of ourselves are often the strongest, right?

May we live so
full that life
decides to choose
us back.

Highest self
highest love
highest health
highest wealth

Highest look
highest feels
highest love
highest hills

Wanna reach my highest
wanna feel my highest.

HOW MANY DEATHS DO WE HAVE IN A LIFETIME?

Curiosity always seems to pull me back, despite my knowing. I convince myself that this connection and I are on the same level, to delay the responsibility of acknowledging that "this ain't it for me."

Delay in cutting the grass blocks the new growth.

The biggest justification we indulge is that of expectation. That since I know what to "expect," I won't be in my feelings this time. But pain finds a way to hurt again. You don't get stronger, you get more closed off, especially when you keep taking their projections and shortcomings as your own.

I've probably died a hundred deaths

disobeying spirit to hold onto expired connections and seasonal people.

We hold onto people, not because we want them, but because we can't forgive them. Can't forgive them for hurting us. Can't forgive them for not being someone who could stay in our lives. Can't forgive them for not showing up for us. Shit, can't forgive ourselves for overlooking the clown shit. The only constant is change, just as the only must for peace is continual forgiveness.

Take your time
with yourself.
You are sacred ground
You are the most
solid person you have.

TODAY, I GOT BY

In a world where I'm so used to fighting for joy,
show me what it's like to rest in it.
Nowadays, I'm just tryna stay happy,
tryna stay tapped into self
because the God in me don't need to worry. The more we pray, the more
faith grows.
But some days be having me in a chokehold.
Getting so used to the lows,
like highs don't exist for me.
Forgetting that life be working in ways to benefit me.

FINDING BALANCE

We cling to certain timelines.

Because of the person we are with, or the person we are within the moment. Either way, our home is left rattled when balance needs to be restored. At that point, there is no room to hide, only a door that we're called to walk through, and there is no choice but to accept the changes afoot.

I'm learning that some transitions are abrupt and some shifts are uncontrollable, but that's when grace becomes my best friend.

Learning to give myself credit for rolling with the punches. For breathing deep through the tears and coaching myself as I collect my bearings. For keeping gratitude as my focus and my heart open. And for acknowledging my ability to forge ahead in this life, even if I have to cry and keep it pushing.

It always teaches more than it hurts.

They never tell us why good things expire and how not to hold out hope for things we still want. They never tell us how to practice trust that something greater is on the way when our hearts are still stuck in the traffic of it all. All that's ever implied is that through attachment we create our own suffering, and that it's wise to lean into faith to activate our power.

However, that faith walk is a bitch. It requires us to drop the bags, with our old house keys, our old routines, and our old ways of thinking, because now it's time to access another part of ourselves, by ourselves. I'm learning that sometimes familiar and safe still have missing parts. Sometimes, they can cause us to "chill" too hard on purpose. And though safe and familiar can lead to something "healthy," at some point we all have to take inventory of our personal growth and goals.

I am a bit wiser now to know that no one "leaves me" or I them, but that I've done all that I could and now I'm being granted access to another part of myself that needs attention outside of the relationship.

I won't allow that to go to waste.

I know that to love unconditionally is to let go, as they say. And to stay in balance is to hold on to myself, as I'm learning. This time, the cling is to myself. To keep me prioritized. That's the only way I know how to keep my head above water, and maybe that's all I need to know right now as I navigate the unknown.

I've had this complex belief that if I loved someone, I would make it work by any means. But although love is the answer, love simply just isn't enough.

How do I move forward? By loving. Loving myself. Loving them. Giving reverence to the relationship that was because it taught me what is. Giving value even in its separation. Honoring what I learned during that time, and then finding a new outlet to transmute those teachings into something I'm passionate about. Far too often, I let sadness sink deep into my chest, forcing my heart to close. But this time I know better.

How do I let go of something that may have been good and safe but that required too much of me during this season of my life? That answer, I don't know. All I can say is that I have to ride the wave, however it comes, with the intention to just hold on to me right now. Unclench my hands, open my palms, and release the grip on anything else. Free it to the water as I move, like so, knowing that what's meant will meet me on the shorelines when it's time.

No rushing timelines. No clinging either. Just finding acceptance in each day and liberating myself with new peace as I go.

In moments of trying to obtain the things I think I want, I am learning more about myself and the things I actually need.

That is the only way. That is the balanced way.

The key to making anything work itself into balance is the same key used to work on ourselves.

I WROTE THIS LISTENING TO
POUND CAKE BY DRAKE

I'm too scared to speak up.
I'm too scared that you might run.
I'm afraid she's coming back,
the girl who begs for love.
I break my own heart
tryna get what I rightfully deserve.
Tryna get it out of people
who never had it to give in return.

Only getting crumbs
for the sake of the peace.
Cool with getting crumbs
outta fear that they might leave,
you take what you can get.
people do this shit with ease.
Tryna find me the one who won't quit on me.
Say she really fuck with me,
say he really fuck with me,
cuz I ain't perfect
but I'm worth it.
Ain't nothing perfect
beneath the surface.
I used to look at you
and see endless love.
Now I look at you
and see the end we avoid to discuss.
Both not ready.

LOVE DON'T ALWAYS SPIN THE BLOCK

It was my birthday. We were coming back from celebrating at this boutique hotel in Brooklyn. I remember my motion sickness was at an all-time high in the passenger seat of your Honda. I remember being mad at you because I knew something was off, we both weren't speaking up on the disconnect, but I couldn't even be mad. We both felt it, but I was battling. You were cool with the silence; I grew annoyed in the quiet. We both could feel it was time to end it. The chapter was closed, we just ignored it because we put so much time in. We were holding on out of fear rather than love. We'd been dancing around the elephant, afraid of how life would look once we decided to walk separate paths.

The air was stiff. Your body was too. I could tell you were attempting to hold your composure just long enough to reach home, put the car in park, and say what it was. I read the energy before I even needed you to say anything. It was a silent agreement before I ever said a word.

I said, "What are we even doing anymore?" We hadn't felt easy for months. We were growing distant, out of love. Out of not wanting to hurt the other, ignoring ourselves to keep the peace. Too afraid to walk away and try for another level of freedom. You were my safe place, you were always there when I needed saving, but I couldn't rest there, we weren't living anymore. We coasted out of habit.

I'm not too proud to admit you were my whole heart for those years and you'll always have a piece, because the love I give is yours to keep. But we outgrew each other–nothing more we could do for one another. We beat it in the ground. The longer you beat something in the ground, you become bad company together. I wasn't good for myself back then, and you weren't good to yourself either.

And that's when we knew it was time. We'll never speak again after this.

Things can still be tender. That doesn't mean you're still stuck on them though.

LET US LIGHT SOME SAGE

I'm in new waters, but I am not seeking shore, because having to be so sure until a move is made is a sure way to live a life that calculates.

Where flow feels forced, I'm forcing myself to do things differently. But ain't that what growth is?

Being uprooted to be replanted feels more like drowning than feeling grounded, but darkness be my best light, my shadows where I shine bright. The deepest parts of me, I no longer keep tight. I let 'em loose. I let 'em free. I let 'em dance. I let 'em be.

I learned a long time ago to take my hands out of the pot when you're cooking with God. When you start playing with the recipe, the blessings get sabotaged. Sometimes the best way to help yourself is to do less to get realigned. Asking questions like: What makes me feel safe and most cared for? What kind of love fills me up on the inside?

I'm more than one thing. I need forehead kisses and gentle touches whisking over my skin like paintbrushes. Soft words in hard conversations that leave me open in vulnerable situations, but I still feel safe in. That love that has infinite patience because I'm impatient but willing to see love from another angle. The love that's willing to see me on all levels because I am more than one thing on any given day.

I don't always look the same, might be in my masculine ways, may need a little grace. But I'm learning to stop letting people play when I know the love would never grow past the games. We peak on the shallow side because mirrors only go as deep as our shadows, right?

Stop going places where you leave with more questions than answers. You traumatize yourself that way.

Tiptoeing fully dressed only gets you half-loved with more stress, and pleasure can only be felt as deeply as you undress. And most of y'all don't even like the reflection staring back.

I suppose I am in a space where I just want enough to be significant, no more than needed. Cutting out the excess, my mind deserves some freedom. To think, to feel, to process in peace. Bringing my body back in rhythm, back home in ease. Every time I make it back safely, I give a flower to all the women I've been, all the versions it took for me to find my way. They all carried me through different prayers I would have still been kneeling for.

I dance carelessly in my garden, so many starting lines, I am just getting started. Wind kissing my face to solidify the commencement of moving forward. Dusting off the ends that lingered until I said no, the very clippings I lay at my altar, giving gratitude for all that they offered. They served me well, until I was well enough to identify what was no longer needed.

My growth brings grief, and balance feels like discomfort when I am no longer identifiable to yesterday and far from as familiar as I was six months ago. I hold space for all the versions of me that I now release into a place where there is no space and time. May reverence hold them more than my memory allows. The people, the connections, the places, the emotions, all of which came with versions of myself that expired.

I pray they make it to someone who can carry them farther than I could.

Your emotions
will make someone
bigger than
they actually are.

Give time a chance
to work on your behalf.

RUBBERBAND PROBLEMS

Life always seems to tug at the seams, right where I am struggling the most. Almost as if its pleasure is to find me unraveled, at full surrender, void of control. I tried everything to quickly sew every stitch just to make something stick, but my fingers bled in desperation.
The stretching is well past its welcome, causing tension that is too much to come back from. Asking myself questions that I should be the master of. How flexible do I have to be before the bend breaks my back?

It really scares me how low I let myself feel to get moving sometimes.

I'm spiraling, but you would never be able to tell because my composure is golden.

"Never let them see you sweat."
Whole time, I'm drenched in worry that my ego won't let go of until I make a quick fix for some ease of thought. I keep telling myself that, knowing the sun will greet me by tomorrow, I have no concerns to drape the sky. But I keep trying to color that motherfucker every time.

"Time will align how it needs to."
Often never soothes, just leaves you questioning when you'll be able to let out a sigh of relief. To be of service makes me feel like I am worth something, so what does it say about me now?
I need more than a second to feel okay for a minute.
Cut out the excess,
my mind deserves some freedom
to think
to feel
to process in peace.
bringing my body back in rhythm,
back home in ease.

A flower given to
all the women
I've been.
They have carried me
from many hells to
answered prayers.

ONGOING NOTHINGNESS

I'm the type you remember when you go to sleep.
Stitched in your every fiber like fabric. Stuck all in your energy. You play it cool, but it's cool, you don't have to tell me. I'm in your head rent free. I have a sixth sense—I feel shit before it makes sense.
We never made sense. We just made mess and called it love.
I cried, we argued. We didn't know a love without painful endurance.
Some parts were beautiful though, really thinking we could move mountains.
Like somehow stepping on each other's toes would lead us to the top hills.
But I gave myself permission to step off the ledge, because love ain't supposed to feel like a slow death.
We were going nowhere fast. Enjoying the fight more than making it right.
We were both wrong for holding on.
I made a habit out of watering the dead, but sometimes we just want what we want.
Sometimes we crave the little things
more than the aloneness we need.
Things like someone to hold you on bad days,
hands cradling your limbs into a prayer for protection.
Sweet reminders that greet your day before the demands have a chance to.
Small surprises like a midday phone call just to say just because.
Feels good, don't it?
To know that someone has a thought wrapped around me like a favorite throwback classic on repeat.
The simple gestures of letting someone stand behind you to pull you close by the waist -
spine to chest -
upholding the weight of each other.

I desire reciprocity
the way the sun exchanges turns with the moon.
I want to dance across time so smooth that it moves on my dime.

I try not to draw lines, but I disrespect myself letting people cross mine.
Too often caught in a crossfire
that confines my mind
I just want to live,
reaching my arms toward the light,
praying it wins
and it drenches over me,
drowning out self-doubt, fear, insecurity, hurt, past pain, unresolved
conversations that I had to bury.

I buried a lot of people before God told me why.

Graveyard shift, it was the only way to get through the nights.
I don't talk about it often.
Laid out all of our secrets,
laid to rest our unfinished business.
Sprinkled in some hugs and well wishes
right with some flowers on the coffin.
I hope you know I wished for different
until wishing was more painful than acceptance.
Ain't no way around it–
There's grieving in everything, but pain brings alignment.

I grieve over people.
I miss their laughs.
I miss their presence.
But I never miss who I was when I was with them.
Growth is a beautiful thing.

I cry rivers,
just to shake the sky
full of laughter.
It all depends on
where I'm standing
that day.

PAY YOUR RESPECTS

I watered the ground with tears I once felt buried under. Thought it was time to pay my respects, to give my flowers. Field full of past trauma, space filled with past lovers.
Old versions lay like corpses
left rotting like most things we run from that's calling for a homecoming.
I guess I'm giving myself permission to revisit a sweet moment to sit in, one that would be a testament to how far I've come.
Old habits die hard, they say,
them wounds don't heal without marks.
It's a slow fade,
and I still have reason to believe peace gonna spin the block for me.

True joy is not dependent on physical sight. It's what we feel in our hearts.

Your heart is full
of gems. Trust it.

ARRIVAL: NEW JOYS, OLD LOVES

There will be days when
my heart will remind me of you.
I'll half-smile and snark at the thought.
I'll immediately swell up with mixed emotion,
rolling my eyes at the bittersweet nostalgia.

I'll look through old photos
and realize how different I am now.
How life fills my cheeks,
how the sun catches my eyes,
how joy found a way to
wiggle through the cracks of my teeth.
And how worthy I feel after picking my head up by the chin and keeping it pushing.

I'll realize how many amazing people I've met and
how many experiences I've had since your departure.

Thierra,
I hope you know there will be days when
you'll forget all your progress and be tempted to isolate into the storm of your mind.
You'll miss people you had no business dealing with in the first place.
You'll cry at nothing.
You'll think about all your past lovers and how different life would have looked had you not been fumbled and saved by the grace of the universe.
You'll give into the tricks of your mind.
You'll overthink out of habit.
You'll let stress override your faith.

Promise me that when you catch yourself having one of those days,
You'll remember that the hardest moments are when Spirit is calling you closer for an even bigger blessing.
Prepare yourself for compensation on the things never meant to stay.
You're one of the lucky ones.
Life is never falling apart, only coming together in new ways.
So live now, live fully.
Do not rob yourself of that.
And most importantly,
remember *love*.
You are covered in it.

www.ingramcontent.com/pod-product-compliance
Lightning Source LLC
Chambersburg PA
CBHW020249010526
44107CB00002B/165